Wolves

NATURE'S PREDATORS

Marcia S. Gresko

KIDHAVEN PRESS™

GALE

San Diego • Detroit • New York • San Francisco • Cleveland
New Haven, Conn. • Waterville, Maine • London • Munich

Cover Page photo: © Layne Kennedy/CORBIS
Associated Press, AP, 39, 40
© Bauer, Erwin & Peggy/Animals Animals/Earth Scenes, 16
© Bettmann/CORBIS, 36
© Jim Brandenburg/Minden Pictures, 15, 24, 29
© Corel Corporation, 19
© Tim Fitzharris/Minden Pictures, 26
© D. Robert & Lorri Franz/CORBIS, 12
© Layne Kennedy/CORBIS, 33
© Michael Mauro/Minden Pictures, 21, 34
Brandy Noon, 7, 9, 38
© Lynda Richardson/CORBIS, 4, 8
© Richard Hamilton Smith/CORBIS, 20
© Jeff Vanuga/CORBIS, 11
© Konrad Wothe/Minden Pictures, 27, 30

© 2003 by KidHaven Press. KidHaven Press is an imprint of The Gale Group, Inc.,
a division of Thomson Learning, Inc.

KidHaven™ and Thomson Learning™ are trademarks used herein under license.

For more information, contact
KidHaven Press
27500 Drake Rd.
Farmington Hills, MI 48331-3535
Or you can visit our Internet site at http://www.gale.com

LIBRARY OF CONGRESS CATALOGING-IN-PUBLICATION DATA

Gresko, Marcia S.
  Wolves / by Marcia S. Gresko.
    p. cm.—(Nature's predators)
  Summary: Introduces different species of wolves, focusing on how they hunt
  and kill other animals.
  Includes bibliographical references and index. (p.   ).
  ISBN 0-7377-1008-X (hardback)
  1. Wolves—Juvenile literature. [1. Wolves.] I. Title. II. Series.
  QL737 .C22 G74   2003
  599 . 773—dc21

  2001008204

Printed in the United States of America

Contents

Chapter 1

Wolf Ways

Two huge, shaggy wolves stare at one another. Suddenly, one leaps toward the other, placing its great forepaws around the other's neck. They growl and wrestle. Separating, the wolves face one another again. Now one drops its front quarters into a crouch position, its thick, bushy tail wagging. The other bounds away, and the friendly chase begins.

Nearby, under the watchful eyes of their mother, the pups also play. One stalks the bees buzzing in the wildflowers. Another parades about with its toys—bison bones and scraps of skin. Two stage a clumsy mock fight, pouncing on one another and snapping fiercely.

The remainder of the **pack** rests. Some doze; others scan the landscape with piercing, golden eyes. It is a peaceful scene.

But as the sun sets, the pack becomes restless. Its largest member, a powerful gray male, sniffs the air. He points his nose skyward and howls. The other wolves dance with excitement. They wag their tails, licking one another, and finally add their voices to the wild song. It is time to hunt.

A Meat Eater's Menu

Wolves are **predators**—animals that kill and eat other animals. Three species of wolves exist: the Abyssinian wolf, the red wolf, and the gray wolf. All wolves are **carnivores**. But what is on the menu depends on where a wolf lives and the types of **prey** that are available.

About five hundred Abyssinian wolves are found in Ethiopia—their only **habitat**. Abyssinian wolves mostly prey on small rodents. However, they will also eat birds, their eggs, or the remains of dead animals. Sometimes Abyssinian wolves hunt young antelope, lambs, or hare.

Red wolves are found only in the United States. Because they are highly **endangered**, most of the approximately three hundred remaining red wolves live in captive breeding facilities. About a third run free in areas in the southeastern United States. In the wild, red wolves eat mainly deer and raccoon, but also rabbits and mice.

Most of the approximately 150,000 wolves in the world are gray wolves. Gray wolves (which range in color from white to black) live in about forty different countries in North America, Europe, and Asia. In North America, most gray wolves inhabit Canada and Alaska, but some live in the northern United

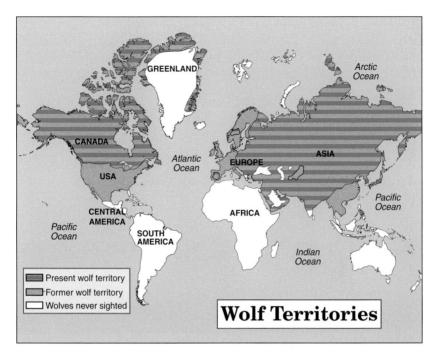

Wolf Territories

Legend:
- Present wolf territory
- Former wolf territory
- Wolves never sighted

Map labels: GREENLAND, Arctic Ocean, CANADA, Atlantic Ocean, EUROPE, ASIA, USA, Pacific Ocean, CENTRAL AMERICA, AFRICA, Pacific Ocean, SOUTH AMERICA, Indian Ocean

States. Gray wolves will eat almost anything from mice to moose, but they seem to like **ungulates**—large, hoofed animals such as deer—best.

The type of ungulate hunted depends on a wolf's habitat. Northern wolves feed on caribou, moose, bison, and musk oxen. Forest-dwelling wolves stalk deer and elk. Wild sheep are on the menu in the mountains. Big animals such as these supply wolves with lots of meat.

In the summer, wolves often hunt alone, gobbling up the many small animals born in the spring. Beaver or rabbits make a good meal then. When its natural prey is scarce, wolves sometimes hunt cattle and other domestic animals. Hungry wolves will devour birds, fish, lizards, snakes—even grasshoppers, earthworms, and berries.

Forest-dwelling gray wolves feed on a large deer.

Hungry as a Wolf

Because gray wolves are large, active animals, they need a lot of food. Males average 5 to 6 ½ feet long and weigh between 70 and 120 pounds. Females are usually about 20 percent smaller. The largest gray wolf on record was a male who weighed 175 pounds—about as much as a full-grown man. To fuel their big bodies, wolves eat an average of 5 to 12 pounds of food per day.

But wolves must often go for several days or even weeks without eating. Finding, chasing, catching, and killing prey is a hard job. Wolves catch and kill their prey only 7 to 10 percent of the time. Most prey escapes.

When a large kill is made, wolves welcome the feast—gorging themselves on as much as twenty pounds of meat in one meal. But wolves digest their food quickly. In just a few hours, they are hungry and ready to hunt again. If prey is plentiful, the wolf will kill and feed again because it does not know when its next meal might be.

Sensational Senses

The wolf's keen senses are important weapons for hunting its next meal. A powerful sense of smell, sensitive hearing, and the ability to detect small movements make the wolf a mighty hunter.

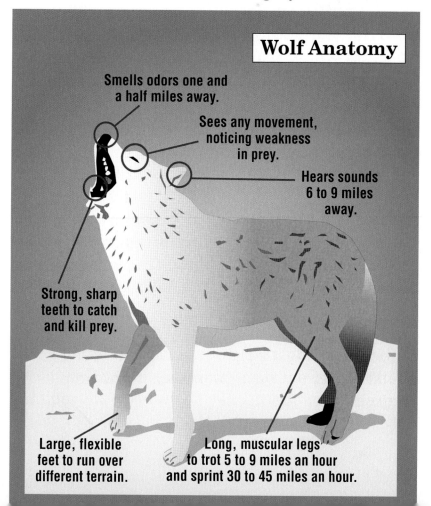

Wolf Anatomy

Smells odors one and a half miles away.

Sees any movement, noticing weakness in prey.

Hears sounds 6 to 9 miles away.

Strong, sharp teeth to catch and kill prey.

Large, flexible feet to run over different terrain.

Long, muscular legs to trot 5 to 9 miles an hour and sprint 30 to 45 miles an hour.

Like other members of the dog family to which it belongs, the wolf has an excellent sense of smell. Researchers estimate a wolf can probably smell one hundred times better than a human can. Its large, long nose is packed with more than 150 million tiny smelling cells. Wolves sniff the air. If the wind is right, they can detect prey 1½ miles away. There are even reports of wolves scenting a moose and her calves grazing more than 4 miles away.

Although wolves usually find their prey by smell, they also use their hearing. With its sharp hearing, a wolf can pick up sounds as far as six miles away in the forest and ten miles away on the open tundra. It can even hear an animal that is buried under the snow.

Sight is a wolf's least developed sense. Wolves smell or hear their prey long before they see it. But, they notice instantly any movement, such as a limp, the prey makes. Wolves use these cues to target weak or old animals.

On the Move

Despite their spectacular senses, wolves may travel more than thirty miles a day searching for food. Luckily, wolves are built for running. In fact, an old Russian saying states, "the wolf is kept fed by its feet."

A wolf's feet are large, blocky, and flexible. This makes them ideal for running over different kinds of terrain—from open plains to dense forests. In deep snow the feet act like snowshoes, allowing the

At full sprint, a gray wolf chases its prey at thirty-five to forty-five miles per hour.

wolf to overtake prey floundering in the snow. On steep, slippery slopes, a wolf's paw sprawls widely, grasping at uneven surfaces as it pursues prey scrambling for the safety of rocky ledges.

A wolf's legs are long and muscular. Usually, a wolf trots along tirelessly at five to nine miles per hour. But it can reach short bursts of speed up to thirty-five to forty-five miles per hour in pursuit of fleet-footed prey. And, as quickly as it starts a chase, a wolf can use its legs as brakes to change direction, dodge, or get ready for another long race.

What Big Teeth You Have

Awesome senses, speed, and stamina enable wolves to catch up to their prey. But their deadliest weapons are their teeth. These are the tools wolves use to catch, kill, and cut up large prey.

Wolves have forty-two teeth, ten more than humans have. Sharp and pointed, they are perfect for grabbing, holding, and tearing flesh. Four knifelike fangs called canines may grow two inches long. Wolves will sink these daggers deep into the rub-

A timber wolf uses its knifelike, canine teeth to tear the flesh of a newly killed doe.

bery nose of a moose, clinging even while the panicked animal raises its head and swings it from side to side.

Wolf Wisdom

Hunting and killing large animals such as moose or bison requires skill and intelligence. Native Americans, who also once depended on these animals for food, clothing, and utensils, respected the wolf's hunting ability and studied its strategy. They honored the wolf in their dances and stories. One of their names for it was "The Teacher."

Wolves are excellent problem solvers. To hide their scent, they sometimes roll in carrion—dead animals. To prevent nimble mountain sheep from escaping, wolves try to approach them from above or on the flat lands between mountain ranges.

Wolves are also keen observers with good memories. Captive wolves have learned to escape from their pens by watching their human keepers unlock the enclosures. In the past, trappers told stories of wolves learning to avoid even the cleverest traps set for them.

Wolves are smart and speedy. They are equipped with spectacular senses and sharp teeth. This combination allows wolves to be at the top of the food chain.

Chapter 2

Fierce Hunter

Although wolves are fierce hunters, ungulates are not "easy prey." One moose can outweigh as many as ten wolves! Fleet-footed deer can leave their pursuers snapping at thin air. Caribou and bison gather in large, protective herds where there are many eyes, ears, and noses to discover prowling wolves. Hunting such prey takes teamwork.

Life in the Pack

Wolves live and hunt together in groups called packs. Packs vary in size from three to as many as twenty or more members. The biggest recorded pack included thirty-six wolves. Most packs have six to ten members. Wolf packs are usually smaller where their prey are smaller, such as deer, and larger where their prey are larger, such as moose.

A pack is a family. It consists of a mother and father and their offspring of various ages. Like a human family, the pack feeds and shelters its mem-

A pack of timber wolves stands over the carcass of a deer. Wolves hunt in packs to bring down large prey.

bers and raises the young—teaching them the skills they need to survive. Packmates are very friendly—grooming one another, sniffing each other's fur, and keeping close by. Playing together is a favorite pastime.

Packs, like families, also need to keep peace and order. If wolves often fight and hurt one another, they might be too injured to hunt. Their survival would be jeopardized. To maintain unity, a

Gray wolf packmates play together, gently biting and nudging each other.

pack is organized by rank. Each member of the pack has its place in the pack's social system, usually related to its age.

The parents, called the **alpha** pair, **dominate** the pack. Older and more experienced, they are the decision makers. They select the pack's home **territory**, choose when and where to hunt, pick which prey to attack, even decide where the pack will sleep at night. When danger threatens, they charge ahead ready to defend the younger wolves from harm. Middle-ranked, or **beta**, wolves control their inexperienced brothers and sisters at the bottom of the social ladder. In a large pack, there is often also an **omega** wolf—picked on by the whole pack. Frequently harassed, feeding on the scraps of the kill, and living on the fringes of pack life, this unlucky animal may be driven away or leave on its own to become a lone wolf.

Each pack inhabits its own territory. Territories range in size depending on the quality of hunting, the number of pack members, and the competition from neighbors. If the hunting is good, wolves may be content to roam in smaller areas—thirty to one hundred square miles. But where prey is scarce, a pack's territory may be huge—one thousand or more square miles. Wolves mark the edges of their territory by leaving urine and **feces** on trees, rocks, and dirt piles. These smelly "no trespassing signs" warn other wolves to keep out. Howling also alerts unwelcome visitors that a territory is taken.

Lone Wolves

Lone wolves are animals that have left the pack to live by themselves. Wolves leave the safety of the pack for different reasons. Some, like omega wolves, are forced out. Others are former leaders of a pack that have lost their position to a younger, stronger member's challenge. Most loners are young wolves who have left the pack to find a mate and territory of their own. Some are successful; others remain lone wolves.

The single life is difficult. Single wolves may bring down large prey. But hunting is easier in a pack.

On the Prowl

Whether wolves hunt alone or with the pack, they must first find their prey. Wolves travel far and wide searching for their meals. The pack usually travels single file with a member of the alpha pair in the lead.

Most often the leaders locate prey by its odor. When they smell an animal, they stop suddenly. The rest of the pack freezes—eyes, ears, and noses pointed toward the prey. Then they set a course directly toward the welcome scent of dinner.

Wolves also use their sensitive noses to track prey. If they discover a fresh game trail they will follow it, noses glued to the ground, hoping it leads to a meal.

Sometimes wolves just get lucky. Where prey is plentiful, they may find animals accidentally. But wolves cannot depend on chance for a steady diet.

Menu Choices

Wolves use a lot of energy locating prey, so they try to make the hunt as easy as possible. Wolves are opportunistic. This means that they look for animals that are sick or injured, weak, or old. A diseased deer or lame moose, a helpless caribou calf that has strayed from the herd, or an elk slowed by age all make perfect targets.

A lone wolf sniffs the air and listens intently for any sound that will lead it to prey.

What seems bloodthirsty is actually helpful. Killing weak animals guarantees the strongest animals remain to have healthier young. Eliminating sick animals helps control the spread of disease. Controlling the size of the herd means that there will be enough food for its members and an overgrown herd will not destroy its habitat.

The Hunt

Once an animal or a herd is discovered, the pack moves toward it. As they get closer, the wolves become excited. They move quickly, wagging their

With its head lowered and legs bent, a wolf slowly stalks its next meal.

tails, and peering eagerly ahead. Ready to leap forward, the wolves remain patient. They slowly sneak nearer. Head lowered, eyes focused on their prey, the wolves try to gain every last inch unnoticed. This careful approach is called the stalk.

If their prey notices them, the wolves freeze. Predators and prey eye each other—waiting tensely for a response. This showdown is called the encounter.

Faced with a hungry pack of wolves, most prey runs for its life. But big, aggressive animals such as moose and bison may stand their ground. When this happens, wolves often do not attack—fearing the angry antlers and pounding hooves of these immense animals. Instead, they try to surround the animal and wait. They act casually. Some may even move off for a playful game. Now and then, one or more of the hungry hunters will charge the animal—trying to stampede it. If the animal refuses to run, the pack usually moves off to look for an easier meal. But if the animal bolts, the wolves begin the rush—the most important stage in the hunt.

A large moose stands its ground against a single wolf. Large, aggressive animals can force a wolf to back down.

During the rush, the wolves spring forward in great bounds. They try to get as close as possible to their fleeing food. If their prey succeeds in gaining a long lead, the wolves are unlikely to catch up with it. Their top-speed rush must gain them enough ground to attack or at least give them a good start during the chase.

Working Together

Once the chase has begun, pack members work together to make a kill. They may place themselves along their prey's escape route and use a kind of relay race plan. As pursuing wolves tire, rested wolves take over until the exhausted animal is brought down. Other times prey are ambushed by hidden wolves or distracted in mid-dash by part of the pack while the rest circles and attacks from the rear.

The chase may last several minutes, or just seconds. It may go on for hours, or on and off for a few days. But most chases are short, and the pack moves in for the kill.

Chapter 3

The Kill

Most prey is attacked on the run. Wolves know that an animal in flight is less able to kick and injure them.

As the wolves catch up to an animal, such as a moose, part of the pack lopes behind, but a few wolves sprint alongside it. Deadly canines bared, they spring toward the moose's rump—a wide, meaty area—far from its front and hind hooves. Slashing and tearing at the rump muscles, the wolves slow the animal down, sink their teeth into it, and try to hang on. The weight of several large predators tugging at its rump may bring the moose down. If not, a wolf, usually one of the alpha pair, will leap at the moose's head and grab it by the nose. The wolf tries to stand with its body stretched out as far away from the moose as possible. While the moose tries to loosen the grip on its nose, the rest of the pack attacks from all sides, biting its neck and throat, shoulders and sides. Finally, the moose sinks to the ground—a victim of blood loss, shock, or both.

Arctic wolves stampede a pack of musk oxen. The wolves bite and tear at the oxen until the animals fall to the ground.

Other large ungulates, such as elk and caribou, are killed in a similar way. Smaller ungulates, such as moose calves, sheep, and deer, can be ridden down by a single wolf. Seizing them by the throat or head, the wolf inflicts a suffocating hold.

Single wolves will also chase rabbits or follow beaver trails. A crushing neck bite is usually enough to snap the backbone of these small prey. Wolves listen for mice and other snack-size rodents hiding under the leaves, too. Then they pounce—trapping the rodents between their large front paws—and gulp them down. These minimeals are good practice for younger, less experienced wolves.

Mealtime

Though the pack has worked as a practiced team to kill its prey, when a meal is on the table, it is a savage scene.

The alpha leaders are the first to eat after a kill has been made. They begin feeding excitedly, claiming the choicest portions of the carcass. They sink their sharp canine teeth into the animal's thick hide and tug, ripping open its belly. Inside are prized portions of the kill—the animal's heart, lungs, and liver. These and other soft organs are a rich store of fat and nutrients. The wolves devour them, leaving uneaten only the undigested food inside their prey's stomach.

Soon the beta animals share the meal. Then the rest of the wolves begin to feed. If the kill is large—a banquet-sized moose—then the entire pack will feast on the carcass. If it is small, some of the lower-ranking wolves must make do with scraps.

Using rows of sharp, pointed teeth, pack members tear at the rump and other wounded areas within their reach. Snarling and snapping, the wolves guard their share of the hard-earned meal. With their specially designed carnassials, or flesh teeth, they carve hunks of meat and hide from the

Three timber wolves fight over a deer carcass.

body. Barely chewing, they use their long, flexible tongues to swallow the food whole. One wolf stomach was reported to hold a caribou's ear, tongue, lip, kidneys, liver, and windpipe, as well as hair and two large chunks of meat!

Wolves eat quickly. The faster they eat, the more food they will get. There are reports of wolves eating twenty pounds of meat in less than two hours.

Once the pack has "wolfed down" the meaty parts of the carcass, they turn to the next course—the bones. Pinning them between their paws, wolves use their front teeth to nip and gnaw meat from the bones. Then they set to work with their tongues. Covered with hundreds of jagged projections called papillae, the wolf's rough tongue enables it to lick every shred of meat from the bones. Finally its powerful jaws finish the job. With a crushing pressure of fifteen hundred pounds per square inch—twice as strong as the bite of a German

A white timber wolf chews on a large antler. After eating the carcass, wolves gnaw meat and marrow from bones and antlers.

shepherd dog—the wolf shatters the bones. The rich, meaty marrow inside is a tasty treat.

The Leftovers

After the pack has eaten its fill, the wolves spend a few hours relaxing and digesting their meal. Wolves live a feast-or-fast lifestyle. When food is available and plentiful, the wolves will gorge on a kill to make up for days of unsuccessful hunting. A wolf's large, simple stomach enables it to digest great quantities of food quickly and efficiently— using every bit of nourishment from the meat, blood, and bones of its prey.

If the kill is small, the pack will usually consume it from tongue to tail and move on, leaving just the skull, backbone, and stomach contents. Nothing is wasted; even the bloody ground is licked. If the prey is large and the wolves have not finished it off immediately, they will return to the carcass, even over several days.

When prey is plentiful, wolves often cache, or hide, food. Sometimes they carry off a chunk of meat from the kill, dig a hole in the dirt or snow, and bury it. Other times they bury regurgitated (partly digested) food. During tough times, they return to their hidden hoard.

Feeding the Pups

But whether times are good or tough, if there are pups to be fed, the entire pack helps out. While the mother nurses and takes care of the pups, the father

Pups eagerly wait for the pack to return with a large meal from the hunt.

and other pack members bring her meat fresh from the kill. Later when the pups are older, members take turns delivering meals to them and to the "pup-sitters" that stayed behind from the hunt.

Any adult wolf returning from the hunt is greeted excitedly by the hungry pups. Swarming around the returning adult, the whining pups lick and nibble at the adult's mouth. They may even try to get their tongue into the adult's mouth. Soon their pestering pays off. The adult arches its back, opens its mouth wide, and coughs up a pile of partly digested meat. The pups gobble up the steaming stew eagerly. Sometimes the adults bring back whole hunks of meat. Or, if the kill is nearby, they may bring the pups to the carcass instead.

When the Wolf Eats, Everyone Eats

Sometimes wolves kill more prey than they can eat. A blizzard is a bonanza for the pack. During deep snow conditions, heavy prey gets stuck in the drifts, and wolves make many kills. In the spring, many large herds of prey animals such as caribou

A large timber wolf stands guard over a deer. When a wolf cannot eat the entire carcass, scavengers will finish it off.

give birth. Their young make plentiful, easy-to-kill meals, too.

When the pack cannot finish a meal, there are plenty of other animals that are ready to pick the carcass clean. **Scavengers** such as coyotes, opossums, wolverines, eagles, and bears are eager to tidy up after the wolves. Ravens, especially, seem to have a bond with wolves. They are the first scavengers to show up—frequently following the pack, and sometimes even feeding at the same time!

Chapter 4

When Predator Becomes Prey

The life of a hunter is filled with danger. In the wild, the average life span of a wolf is seven or eight years. A lucky wolf may live to the age of nine or ten. Injury, starvation, disease, and violent death are part of daily life. Less than half of wolf pups survive to adulthood.

In Pursuit of Powerful Prey

Pursuing powerful prey is risky business. Charging headlong over rough country is hazardous. Wolves risk stabbing by tree snags, tumbling from rocky ledges, and drowning in fast-flowing rivers.

Once cornered, many prey fight back. One kick from a deer's pointed front hooves can pierce a wolf's body. An elk's antlers can gore it to death. Powerful blows from the rear hooves of a twelve hundred pound moose can shatter a wolf's ribs or crush its skull. Dinner may come at a heavy price—death or a crippling injury. Studies on dead wolves report that nearly 100 percent show some type of old injury, such as a fractured skull, leg, or shoulder.

Animal Enemies

Wolves are not the only predators stalking their dinner either. Hunting eight to ten hours a day, wolves face competition for their meals. Most competitors, from coyotes to cougars, turn tail and run.

A hole in a wolf's skull reveals where a deer landed a powerful kick.

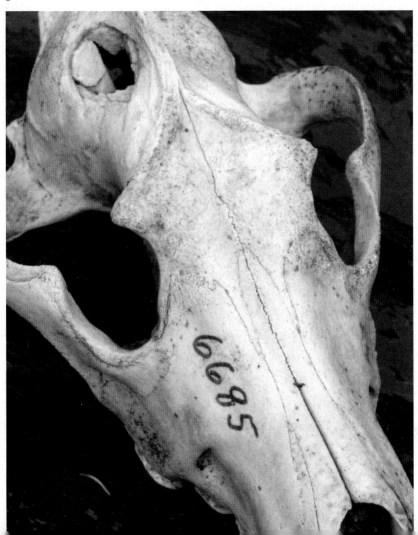

A large grizzly bear defends a moose carcass that he stole from a pack of hungry wolves.

But bears are fearless. Weighing from six hundred to more than one thousand pounds, with long, sharp claws and massive teeth, bears will take over a pack's kill and eat their fill—swatting at the wolves that snap at their heels. Grizzly bears have been known to kill and eat wolf pups. Golden eagles and hawks will also carry off unprotected pups that stray from the **den**.

Other Wolves

Healthy, adult wolves have more to fear from their own kind than they do from other animals. While wolves from the same pack may sometimes battle bitterly for control of the pack, they rarely kill one another. But wolves from different packs will kill one another over territory. If wolves from one pack find a neighboring pack or strange wolf in their territory, they will chase the trespassers, often attacking and killing them. It is hard enough finding food for themselves without sharing it with intruders.

Lone wolves lead the most dangerous lives. Homeless and without the protection of a pack, they are more likely to be killed as trespassers.

The Human Threat

The wolf's deadliest territorial battle has been with humans. Once, wolves were the most widely distributed mammals, except for humans, in the world. They lived in regions from the icy Arctic to the sizzling desert. But as human populations grew and spread into wild areas, wolves' territory shrunk. Today, wolves have been wiped out of most of their former **range** and forced into rough, distant regions of the world—pushed there by humans.

The War on Wolves

European farmers feared and hated wolves, mistakenly believing they were bloodthirsty killers of children and **livestock**. The farmers bred huge dogs, called wolfhounds, just for killing wolves. Farmers even burned down whole forests to destroy the wolves inhabiting them. In some places, citizens could even pay their taxes in wolf heads.

Fairy tales like *Little Red Riding Hood* created a bad opinion of wolves among European settlers in North America.

Later, European settlers arrived in North America. Raised on fairy tales such as *Little Red Riding Hood,* settlers brought their grudge against the wolf with them. The newcomers claimed the wilderness areas—built cities, cleared forests for farms, and turned the prairie into pasture. They killed many of the wolves' usual prey—bison, elk, and deer. As the wolves' hunting grounds disappeared and their natural food supply landed on the dinner tables of human hunters, hungry wolves killed what was available—the settlers' cattle, sheep, and pigs.

The angry settlers declared war on the wolf. Wolves were shot, trapped, and poisoned. Dens were dug up, and the pups were beaten to death or shot. States offered **bounties** for wolves, and professional wolf hunters, called "**wolfers**," made their living by killing them.

By the 1930s the war was over. It is estimated that between 1 and 2 million wolves were killed. As a species, the wolf was nearly **extinct** in the lower forty-eight states.

The Return of the Wolf

For most of the rest of the century, wolves were rarely seen. But in 1973, the Endangered Species Act was passed. It was one of the most important environmental laws of the century. Among its many provisions, it made the killing of wolves anywhere in the United States, except Alaska, illegal. It made returning wolves to their original habitats a goal.

Yellowstone National Park seemed a natural place to restore the gray wolf. Before the last wolves were shot to extinction there in 1926, wolves had lived in Yellowstone for nearly one thousand years. But it would take more than twenty years for wolves to return to the park.

During that time, disagreement and debate raged. Farmers and ranchers insisted wolves would kill their livestock. Hunters complained that wolves would kill the game that hunters pursued for sport. Ignoring the fact that a healthy wolf has never killed a human being in North America, both groups warned about the danger to park visitors.

Finally in January 1995, after years of study, preparation, and legal battles, Operation Wolfstock began. The United States Fish and Wildlife Service trapped fourteen Canadian gray wolves and moved

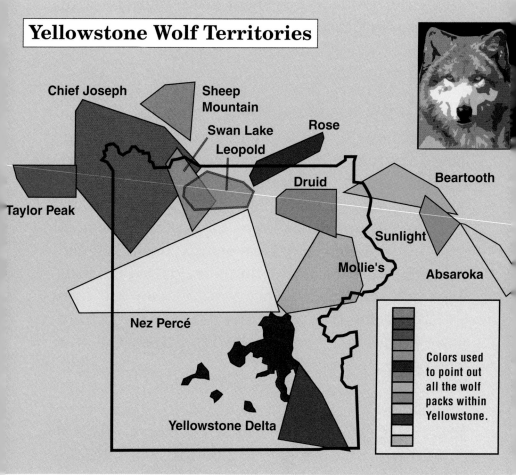

Yellowstone Wolf Territories

Chief Joseph

Sheep Mountain

Swan Lake

Rose

Leopold

Druid

Beartooth

Taylor Peak

Sunlight

Mollie's

Absaroka

Nez Percé

Colors used to point out all the wolf packs within Yellowstone.

Yellowstone Delta

Source: Yellowstone National Park.

them to pens in Yellowstone to get used to their new environment. In March, they were released. Seventeen more Canadian gray wolves were brought to the park the following year, given time to adjust, and released.

Today more than 170 wolves in as many as eighteen packs roam the Yellowstone wilderness. In neighboring Idaho, where wolves were released during the same period, about two hundred wolves now wander free.

Conservation Efforts

This dramatic comeback is the result of several factors. Legal protection, changing public opinion, and the wolf's amazing adaptability have all played an important role. Still, significant challenges remain.

Convincing wary ranchers that they can live peacefully alongside their new neighbors is a tough task. But compromises have enabled both sides to meet their goals. Defenders of Wildlife, a national wildlife advocacy group, pays ranchers for their livestock losses. "Nuisance wolves" that kill livestock are relocated or destroyed—a necessary price for sharing the wilderness with the rest.

Members of the U.S. Fish and Wildlife Service watch as three wolves are returned to the wild.

Erasing myths about wolves is another battle. Wolf research centers and sanctuaries such as the International Wolf Center in Minnesota are in the forefront of the public education effort. Visitors to the center can participate in field trips to find wolf tracks and abandoned dens, evening hikes to hear wolves howl, even guided wolf-research experiments. Nationwide public education programs such as National Wolf Awareness Week in October increase public knowledge and support of wolf preservation.

Certain highly endangered wolf populations—such as the Mexican gray wolf—are currently at great risk. Wolf centers and zoos are meeting this crisis with captive breeding programs, ensuring that even if wolves' natural population is destroyed, the species will not become extinct.

Two red wolf pups bred in captivity sleep in a laboratory at Brevard Zoo in Melbourne, Florida.

Finally, if the wolf is to survive it must have wilderness areas where it can live undisturbed. Environmentalists, from researchers to campers, have joined forces to protect remaining wilderness areas and to lobby for new ones. Their efforts have paid off.

Today, gray wolves in the United States live in Michigan, Wisconsin, Montana, Wyoming, Idaho, Washington, and Minnesota, as well as in Alaska. They remain on the endangered species list in every state except for Minnesota, where they are considered **threatened**, and Alaska, where the population is stable.

Although wolves will never wander freely throughout this country again, their future is brighter than it has been for centuries. Those who have heard their haunting chorus are thankful.

Glossary

alpha: The dominant member (or pair) of a pack.

beta: The middle-ranked wolves.

bounty: Prize money, usually offered for killing something.

carnivore: An animal that eats meat.

den: A shelter, often a small cave or hole dug in the ground to protect the mother wolf and her young pups from the weather and from other animals.

dominate: To be in charge of.

endangered: Referring to a species currently in danger of extinction.

extinct: No longer in existence.

feces: An animal's solid waste.

habitat: The natural environment of a species.

livestock: Animals that are domesticated and raised on a farm or ranch, such as cattle, sheep, and horses.

omega: The lowest-ranking member in the social order of a wolf pack.

pack: A group of animals that gathers together to make hunting and other ways of surviving easier.

predators: Animals that hunt and kill other animals.

prey: An animal that is hunted and eaten by another animal.

range: The geographic area on which a species lives.

scavenger: An animal that finds and eats animals that are already dead.

territory: An area occupied by a pack of wolves.

threatened: Referring to a species that could readily become endangered in the future.

ungulates: Hoofed animals such as deer, moose, bison, and cattle.

wolfers: Hunters who were hired to kill wolves in the United States during the last half of the nineteenth century.

For Further Exploration

Books

Jim Brandenburg, *To the Top of the World: Adventures with Arctic Wolves*. New York: Walker, 1993. A noted wildlife photographer recounts the summer he spent living among a pack of Arctic wolves.

Karen Dudley, *Wolves* (The Untamed World). Austin, TX: Raintree Steck-Vaughn, 1997. Discusses wolves' physical characteristics, habitat, food, reproduction, and pack life. Myths and folklore and a list of "Twenty Interesting Facts" are included.

L. David Mech, *The Way of the Wolf*. Stillwater, MN: Voyager Press, 1991. Outstanding photographs accompany the comments of L. David Mech, renowned wolf biologist and researcher who has studied wolves for more than forty years.

Roland Smith, *Journey of the Red Wolf*. New York: Cobblehill Books/Dutton, 1996. This book is an exciting behind-the-scenes account of the effort to save the red wolf—a species nearly driven to extinction.

Stephen R. Swinburne, *Once A Wolf: How Wildlife Biologists Fought to Bring Back the Gray Wolf.* Boston: Houghton Mifflin, 1999. Traces the persecution of the wolf throughout history, and details the efforts of scientists to reintroduce gray wolves to areas such as Yellowstone National Park.

Periodicals

National Geographic World, "Wolves: Home Free . . . But for How Long?" May 1998.

Karen Rispin, "Peter and the Pack," *Ranger Rick*, January 1991.

Time for Kids, "The Packs Are Back," January 23, 1998.

U.S. Kids, "Hear Them Howl," September 1992.

Websites

The BoomerWolf Page (www.boomerwolf.com). This website provides information, photographs, audio and video clips, and fun, interactive games that teach kids about wolves.

Defenders of Wildlife (www.defenders.org). This national conservation group's website is packed with information about a variety of species, including the wolf. Their kids' site (www.kidsplanet.org) has excellent fact sheets on wolf species, an interactive world wolf population map, and a quiz.

The International Wolf Center (www.wolf.org). This nonprofit organization maintains a wolf sanctuary and research center in Ely, Minnesota. A wolf-cam allows you a view of the residents in one of the center's enclosures.

North American Wolf Association (www.nawa.org). This nonprofit Native American organization is dedicated to the reintroduction and preservation of wolves. In addition to information, there are beautiful photographs and a collection of Native American wolf legends.

Wolf Haven International (www.wolfhaven.org). Wolf Haven International is a nonprofit organization dedicated to wolf protection and restoration projects. The site offers fact sheets on hunting strategy, behavior, communication, pack structure, and conservation issues.

The Wolf Education and Research Center (www.wolfcenter.org). This organization is dedicated to providing public education and scientific research concerning the gray wolf and its habitat in the northern Rocky Mountains. The "Wolf Wisdom" portion of the site offers information about wolf history, pack interactions, wolf communication, and more.

Index